FEARLESS WEALTH

Step-by-Step Guide for Ambitious Christian Women and Mums to Build Wealth and Achieve Their Dreams

PRISCILLA MAKOPA

ISBN: 978-1-916691-97-1

Author services by Opulent Book www.OpulentBooks.net

TABLE OF CONTENTS

Introduction

As women, we wear many hats. We are mothers, wives, business owners, and often everything in between. It is easy to feel like we have to do it all, and do it perfectly. But here is the truth: we cannot pour from an empty cup. Too often, we push ourselves to the brink of exhaustion, trying to grow our businesses, support our families, and maintain a relationship with God, all while fighting feelings of guilt and overwhelm.

I have been there.

There was a time when I was running my business on a six-figure income, and while I believed I could grow it further, I was stuck. My staff were not helping in the way I needed, and I found myself doing almost everything: handling operations, finance, managing staff, and still trying to spend quality time with my children. I was exhausted, working late into the night after everyone had gone to bed and then waking up early to take the kids to school. I felt like I was constantly overworking.

But it was not just the long hours that were taking their toll. I was missing out on precious moments with my children. I felt guilty every time I had to cancel plans for their school events or leave them early for work. I even started missing out on time with my husband. My home life became chaotic, and worst of all, I felt disconnected from the very things that mattered most to me.

Then, it all came crashing down when I lost a major contract. I was faced with the possibility of losing everything my business, my home, and the stability I had worked so hard to create for my family. Fear consumed me. I was at my breaking point, questioning everything, including my business and my calling.

But that was the moment I turned to God for help. I cried out to Him in my despair, and He revealed a way forward. A way to grow my business, have quality time with my children, and find peace in my life. It was not an overnight transformation, but with God's guidance, I developed a proven system that helped me reclaim my time, my energy, and my joy.

This book is for you if you are tired of feeling guilty and overwhelmed and still want to grow your business while having quality time with your family. It is for you whether you are a married woman trying to balance business and family life or a single mum on the same journey. It is also for the woman who is just starting out and battling fear of the unknown. I want you to know that it is possible to grow your business, enjoy family time, and nurture your relationship with God without burning out. You do not have to choose between success and happiness. You can have both.

In the pages that follow, I will share with you the lessons I learned, the strategies I put into practice, and the mindset shifts that helped me break free from the constant cycle of stress. This is a journey I know you can take too. Together, we will work through the steps of building a successful business while maintaining peace, balance, and joy in your life.

You are not alone in this. You can do this, and I am here to show you how.

CHAPTER 1

CREATE A CLEAR VISION

Having a clear vision is like holding a map in your hands before you start a journey. It shows you where you want to go. For an ambitious business woman, this is not just about financial success. It is about creating a life that feels whole and fulfilling. It is about building a thriving business while also being present for your family and nurturing your faith. Without a clear vision, it is easy to get lost in the day-to-day demands of running a business and raising a family. You can become busy but not productive, pulled in a dozen different directions by opportunities that seem good but do not align with what truly matters to you.

A clear vision acts as your filter. It helps you make decisions, big and small, that move you closer to your goals. For example, if one of your core desires is to have more quality time with your children, your vision will guide you to structure your business in a way that supports this. You might choose to delegate certain tasks, outsource specific functions, or set firm boundaries around your working hours. These are not signs of weakness; they are acts of a wise leader who understands that true success is not just about profit margins, but about living a life in alignment with your deepest values.

When your vision is clear, you experience a sense of peace and focus. The constant noise of the world, the endless opportunities, and the pressures to be everything to everyone begin to fade. You are no longer just reacting to circumstances; you are proactively creating the life you desire. This clarity reduces stress because you are not constantly second-guessing your decisions. You know that each step you take, no matter how small, is part of a larger plan to achieve your dream goals and build a life that you genuinely love.

My own journey into entrepreneurship was born from a deeply personal and painful experience. In 2014, my husband helped me start a business providing care for elderly people in their own homes. This was not just a business idea: it was a mission that came straight from my heart. I had watched my own grandmother spend her final days in a hospital, and because of the distance and circumstances, I was never able to say goodbye. That experience left a permanent mark on me. I was determined to create a service that would allow other families to avoid that same pain. I wanted to help elderly people stay in the comfort and familiarity of their own homes, surrounded by their loved ones.

This vision was my driving force. It was not about making money;

it was about making a difference. It was about honouring the memory of my grandmother by ensuring that other families could be present with their loved ones during their most vulnerable times. This heartfelt vision gave me the strength to push through the inevitable challenges of starting a new business. It was my anchor in the storms of financial uncertainty and the demands of juggling business ownership with raising a young family. When you have a vision that is deeply connected to your personal story and your core values, it provides a source of resilience that money alone can never buy.

Your Vision Comes from God

As a woman of faith, it is essential to recognise that your vision for your business and your life is not something you have to create from scratch. It is a gift from God. He is the ultimate leader of your vision, the one who plants the seeds of purpose in your heart. In Deuteronomy 7, we are reminded of God's faithfulness and His covenant with those who love Him. And in Deuteronomy 8:17-18, we are warned against the pride that can come with success: "You may say to yourself, 'My power and the strength of my hands have produced this wealth for me.' But remember the Lord your God, for it is he who gives you the ability to produce wealth."

This is a powerful truth that can transform the way you approach your business. When you understand that your vision is a divine assignment, it takes the pressure off you to have it all figured out. Your role is not to create the vision, but to receive it, nurture it, and walk in obedience to it. This means spending time in prayer, seeking God's guidance, and listening for His voice. It means surrendering your own plans and ambitions to His will, trusting that He has a plan for you that is far greater than anything you could imagine on your own.

One of the greatest challenges for any entrepreneur is the constant stream of opportunities that come their way. Not all of these opportunities are from God. In fact, some of them can be distractions that lead you away from your true calling. This is where discernment becomes so critical. Discernment is the ability to distinguish between what is good and what is best, between what is a genuine opportunity from God and what is simply a temptation to stray from your path. It is a skill that is honed through a close relationship with God, through a deep understanding of His Word, and through a commitment to seeking His will in all things.

When you are faced with a new opportunity, take the time to pray about it. Consider the following:

- Ask God if it aligns with the vision He has given you.
- Does it fit with your values?
- Will it move you closer to your long-term goals?
- Does it bring you a sense of peace, or does it create a feeling

of unease and confusion?

Learning to recognise the voice of God and the subtle nudges of the Holy Spirit is one of the most important skills you can develop as a Christian business owner. It will save you from countless wrong turns and protect you from the heartache of pursuing opportunities that were never meant for you.

The Danger of a Vague Vision

Many of us start our entrepreneurial journeys with a vague sense of what we want to achieve. We want "success", "financial freedom", or "more time with our families". While these are admirable desires, they are not a vision. They are wishes. A true vision is specific, detailed, and deeply personal. It is a clear picture of the future you want to create, a future that you can see, feel, and almost taste.

Without this clarity, we are susceptible to what I call "vision drift." We get pulled off course by the latest trends, the loudest opinions, and the most appealing opportunities. We start chasing someone else's definition of success, and we wake up one day feeling unfulfilled and disconnected from our original purpose. This is a particularly dangerous trap for ambitious women, who are often conditioned to be people-pleasers and to put the needs of others before their own. We can get so caught up in meeting the expectations of our clients, our employees, and our families that we lose sight of our own dreams.

A vague vision also makes it impossible to set meaningful goals. If you do not know where you are going, how can you create a roadmap to get there? You end up with a long to-do list of tasks that keep you busy but do not necessarily move you forward. You work hard, but you do not see the results you desire. This can lead to feelings of frustration, overwhelm, and even burnout. You start to question your abilities and wonder if you are truly cut out for entrepreneurship. The problem is not your work ethic; it is your lack of a clear and compelling vision.

Crafting Your Personal Vision Statement

So, how do you move from a vague wish to a clear and powerful vision? It starts with taking the time to get quiet and listen to your own heart. This is not a luxury; it is a necessity. You cannot hear the voice of God or the whispers of your own soul in the midst of a chaotic and noisy life. You must create space for reflection and introspection.

Here are some practical steps you can take to craft your personal vision statement:

1. **Write Down Your "Big Why."** What is the driving force behind your desire to build a business? What is the change you want to see in the world? What is the legacy you want to leave behind? Do not be afraid to dig deep and get to

the emotional core of your motivation. Your "Big Why" is the fuel that will keep you going when times get tough.

2. **Describe Your Ideal Life.** What does success look like for you and your family? Be as specific as possible. Where do you live? What does your daily routine look like? How do you spend your time? What kind of relationships do you have? What kind of impact are you making? Write it all down in vivid detail. The more clearly you can picture your ideal life, the more real it will become.

3. **Identify Your Core Values.** What are the non-negotiable principles that guide your life? What do you stand for? What is most important to you? Your core values are the foundation of your vision. They are the filter through which you will make all of your decisions. When your actions are in alignment with your values, you will experience a sense of integrity and peace.

4. **Release Your Fears and Anxieties.** Fear is the enemy of vision. It tells you that you are not good enough, that you do not have what it takes, and that you are destined to fail. You must actively combat these fears with faith and truth. Trust that you are on the right path, and that God has equipped you with everything you need to fulfil your calling. Surround yourself with positive and supportive people who will speak life into your dreams.

A Vision for Every Area of Your Life

Your vision should not be limited to your business. It should encompass every area of your life: your family, your faith, your health, and your personal growth. A holistic vision will help you create a life that is not only successful but also sustainable. It will prevent you from sacrificing your well-being or your relationships on the altar of your ambition.

Take the time to create a vision for each of these areas:

- **Family:** What kind of mother and wife do you want to be? What kind of family culture do you want to create? What are your non-negotiable family commitments?
- **Faith:** How do you want to grow in your relationship with God? What spiritual disciplines do you want to cultivate? How do you want to use your business to glorify God?
- **Health:** What are your goals for your physical, mental, and emotional well-being? How will you prioritise self-care and rest? What habits do you need to develop to support your health?
- **Personal Growth:** What skills do you want to learn? What books do you want to read? What experiences do you want to have? How will you continue to grow and evolve as a person?

By creating a vision for every area of your life, you are setting yourself up for true and lasting success. You are building a life that is not only prosperous but also purposeful, a life that is in alignment with your deepest values and your highest calling. This is the foundation of fearless wealth, and it is the first and most important step on your journey to building a life that you love.

Living Your Vision Daily

Crafting a beautiful vision statement is a powerful exercise, but it is only the beginning. The real magic happens when you start to live that vision every single day. Your vision should not be a document that you create once and then file away. It should be a living, breathing part of your daily life, a constant source of inspiration and guidance.

One of the most effective ways to keep your vision at the forefront of your mind is to create a vision board. A vision board is a collage of images, words, and quotes that represent your ideal life. It is a visual representation of your dreams and aspirations. You can create a physical vision board using a corkboard or a poster board, or you can create a digital vision board using a tool like Pinterest. The key is to place your vision board somewhere you will see it every day, such as your office, your bedroom or even your bathroom mirror. This constant visual reminder will help to program your subconscious mind for success and keep you focused on your goals.

Another powerful practice is to review your vision statement every morning. Before you check your email or get caught up in the demands of the day, take a few moments to read your vision statement aloud. This simple act will help to set the tone for your day and remind you of what is truly important. It will help you to be more intentional in your actions and to make choices that are in alignment with your long-term goals.

It is also important to share your vision with the people who matter most to you. When your family, your friends, and your team understand what you are trying to achieve, they can become your greatest supporters. They can encourage you when you are feeling discouraged, hold you accountable to your commitments, and celebrate your successes with you. Do not be afraid to be vulnerable and to share your dreams with others. You will be amazed at how much support you receive when you are willing to open up and let people in.

When Your Vision is Tested

There will be times when your vision is tested. You will face setbacks, disappointments, and failures. You will be tempted to give up and to settle for a life that is less than what you dreamed of. It is in these moments that your vision will become your greatest asset. It will be the anchor that holds you steady in the midst of the storm. It will be the light that guides you through the darkness.

I have faced many moments in my own journey when my vision was tested. I have been betrayed by trusted employees, faced financial hardship, and struggled with the overwhelming demands of being a mother and a business owner. There were times when I wanted to quit, times when I felt like I could not go on. But in those moments, I would remember my "Big Why." I would remember the reason I started my business in the first place: to honour my grandmother and to help other families avoid the pain that I had experienced. That vision gave me the strength to keep going, to fight for my dreams, and to never give up.

Your vision will do the same for you. It will give you the courage to face your fears, the resilience to overcome your challenges, and the determination to achieve your goals. It will be the source of your strength, your hope, and your inspiration. So, I encourage you to take the time to create a clear and compelling vision for your life. It is the most important work you will ever do. It is the foundation of your success, your happiness, and your fearless wealth.

CHAPTER 2
TAKE ACTION

A vision, no matter how clear and compelling, remains a dream until you take action. It is the bridge between where you are and where you want to be. For many ambitious business women, this is where the struggle intensifies. The clarity of vision can be exhilarating, but the path to achieving it can seem daunting, even impossible. The sheer scale of the dream can lead to paralysis, a state of being so overwhelmed by the magnitude of the goal that you do not know where to begin. This is the point where many give up, convinced that their vision is nothing more than a fantasy. But the secret to achieving great things is not found in giant leaps of faith, but in small, consistent, and intentional steps.

Imagine trying to build a house. If you focus on the finished product like the walls, the roof, the windows, the intricate details of the interior, you will quickly become discouraged. The task will seem too vast, too complex. But if you focus on laying one brick at a time, perfectly and with care, you will eventually build a magnificent house. The same is true for your business and your life. The key is to break down your grand vision into small, manageable, and achievable daily actions. These small wins create momentum, build confidence, and steadily move you closer to your ultimate destination.

This principle is beautifully illustrated by the image of a small snowball rolling downhill. At first, it takes effort to get it moving. You have to pack the snow together, give it a push, and guide it in the right direction. But as it begins to roll, it gathers more snow, grows in size, and picks up speed. Soon, it becomes an unstoppable force, a powerful avalanche of progress. This is the power of small, intentional, daily actions. What starts as a seemingly insignificant effort can compound over time into something truly remarkable. This approach demystifies the process of achieving your dreams. It takes them out of the realm of the far-off and unreachable and brings them into the realm of the doable. With each small step you take, you prove to yourself that you are capable, that you are making progress, and that your vision is not just a possibility, but an inevitability.

The Myth of the Overnight Success

Our culture is obsessed with the idea of overnight success. We are bombarded with stories of entrepreneurs who seem to have come out of nowhere and achieved phenomenal success in a short period of time. We see the glamorous results of the multi-million-dollar businesses, the luxurious lifestyles, the adoring fans, but we rarely see the years of hard work, the countless setbacks, and the unwavering commitment that went into achieving those results. This creates a distorted and unrealistic expectation of what it takes to build a successful business.

When we believe in the myth of the overnight success, we become impatient and easily discouraged. We expect to see immediate results, and when we do not, we assume that we are doing something wrong. We start to compare ourselves to others, and we fall into the trap of thinking that everyone else has it figured out except for us. This can be a toxic and destructive mindset, one that can sabotage our efforts and lead us to give up on our dreams prematurely.

The truth is that there is no such thing as an overnight success. Every successful entrepreneur has a story of struggle, perseverance, and relentless action. They have all faced moments of doubt, fear, and uncertainty. They have all made mistakes, experienced failures, and been tempted to quit. The only thing that separates them from those who have given up is that they kept going. They kept taking action, even when they did not feel like it, even when they were not seeing the results they wanted, and even when the odds were stacked against them.

This is a lesson I had to learn the hard way. When I first started my business, I was full of passion and enthusiasm. I had a clear vision of what I wanted to achieve, and I was convinced that I could make it happen quickly. But the reality was much different. I faced financial challenges, marital stress, and the constant struggle of balancing my business with the needs of my young children. There were times when I felt like I was driving a car with a flat tyre, just trying to survive. We were living on quick meals, and there were moments when I struggled to even provide for my children's basic needs.

During this time, it would have been easy to give up. It would have been easy to believe that my vision was just a pipe dream, that I was not cut out for entrepreneurship. But I refused to let go of my dream. I kept taking action, one small step at a time. I kept praying, I kept learning, and I kept pushing forward. It was not glamorous and it was not easy, but it was the only way to turn my vision into a reality. And slowly but surely, things began to change. The small, consistent actions I was taking began to compound, and I started to see the fruits of my labour. It was a long and arduous journey, but it taught me the invaluable lesson that success is not a destination; it is a process of continuous action.

The Power of a Plan

Taking action without a plan is like trying to navigate a ship without a rudder. You will be at the mercy of the winds and the currents, and you will have no control over your destination. A plan is what gives your actions direction and purpose. It is what ensures that you are not just busy, but productive. It is what transforms your vision from a vague dream into a concrete set of goals and objectives.

A good plan starts with your long-term vision and works backward. It breaks down your big goals into smaller, more manageable milestones. It identifies the key strategies you will use to achieve those milestones, and it outlines the specific actions you will take on a daily, weekly, and monthly basis. This process of deconstruction makes your goals feel less intimidating and more achievable. It gives you a clear roadmap to follow, and it allows you to track your progress along the way.

Here is a simple framework you can use to create your action plan:

1. **Set Quarterly Goals.** At the beginning of each quarter, identify the 3-5 most important goals you want to achieve in the next 90 days. These goals should be specific, measurable, achievable, relevant, and time-bound (SMART). They should also be in alignment with your long-term vision.

2. **Break Down Your Goals into Monthly Milestones.** For each of your quarterly goals, identify the key milestones you will need to hit each month to stay on track. These milestones will serve as your checkpoints, allowing you to assess your progress and make any necessary adjustments to your plan.

3. **Create Weekly Action Steps.** At the beginning of each week, review your monthly milestones and identify the specific action steps you will take that week to move closer to your goals. Be as specific as possible. Instead of saying, "work on my marketing," say, "write two blog posts, schedule my social media content for the week, and reach out to three potential collaborators."

4. **Schedule Your Actions.** Once you have identified your weekly action steps, schedule them in your calendar. Treat these appointments with yourself as seriously as you would treat an appointment with a client. This will ensure that you are making time for the most important tasks, the ones that will actually move your business forward.

5. **Review and Adjust.** At the end of each week, take some time to review your progress. Celebrate your wins, and identify any challenges you faced. Use this information to adjust your plan for the following week. This process of continuous review and adjustment is what will keep you on track and ensure that you are always moving in the right direction.

The Importance of Asking for Help

One of the biggest mistakes that entrepreneurs make is trying to do everything themselves. We are often driven by a fierce sense of independence and a desire to prove that we can do it all on our own. But this is a recipe for burnout and failure. The truth is that no one achieves success alone. We all need help, support, and guidance along the way.

Asking for help is not a sign of weakness; it is a sign of strength and wisdom. It shows that you are self-aware enough to recognise your own limitations, and that you are humble enough to learn from others. When you try to do everything yourself, you are limiting your own potential. You are robbing yourself of the opportunity to benefit from the knowledge, skills, and experience of others. You are also creating an unnecessary amount of stress and pressure for yourself.

I learned this lesson the hard way. For a long time, I was the embodiment of "fake it till you make it." I was so afraid of being judged or discouraged that I kept all of my struggles to myself. I acted as if I had it all figured out, even when I was falling apart on the inside. This fear of vulnerability kept me isolated and stuck. It was not until I finally found the courage to ask for help that things began to change.

I found a mentor, a wise and experienced woman who had been where I was and had come out the other side. I shared my challenges with her, my fears, and my dreams. She listened without judgment, and she offered me the guidance and support I so desperately needed. She helped me to see that I was not alone, and that my struggles were not a sign of failure, but a normal part of the entrepreneurial journey. That relationship was a turning point for me. It taught me the invaluable lesson that you can only grow if you are willing to ask for help.

The story of Moses in the Bible provides a powerful illustration of this principle. When God called Moses to lead the Israelites out of Egypt, Moses was full of self-doubt and fear. He did not believe that he was capable of such a monumental task. But God did not expect him to do it alone. He gave him a helper, his brother Aaron, to be his spokesperson. And later, when Moses was overwhelmed by the burden of judging the people, his father-in-law, Jethro, advised him to delegate the task to other capable men. These helpers were essential to Moses' success. Without them, he would have been crushed by the weight of his responsibility.

Just like Moses, we all need divine helpers in our lives. We need mentors who can offer us guidance and wisdom. We need accountability partners who can keep us on track and challenge us to be our best. We need a team of people who share our vision and who are committed to helping us achieve it. And most importantly, we need to be willing to ask for their help. We need to let go of our pride and our fear, and we need to embrace the power of community.

The Power of Prayer in Business Decisions

As a Christian business owner, you have a secret weapon that many others do not: the power of prayer. Prayer is not just a spiritual discipline, it is a powerful tool for business success. When you invite God into your business, you are tapping into a source of wisdom, guidance, and strength that is far greater than your own.

Too often, we try to separate our faith from our work. We go to church on Sunday, and then we leave God at the door when we go to work on Monday. But God wants to be involved in every area of our lives, including our businesses. He cares about our successes and our failures, our hopes and our fears. He wants to be our partner, our guide, and our provider.

When you make prayer a central part of your business practice, you will begin to see a profound shift in the way you make decisions. Instead of relying solely on your own understanding, you will learn to seek God's wisdom. Instead of being driven by fear and anxiety, you will learn to trust in His provision. And instead of feeling like you are carrying the weight of the world on your shoulders, you will learn to surrender your burdens to Him.

I have made it a practice to set aside at least one day a week to review my business plans in prayer. I bring my goals, my challenges, and my decisions to God, and I ask for His guidance. I listen for His voice, and I wait for His peace. This practice has been transformative for my business. It has saved me from making countless mistakes, and it has given me the confidence to move forward with boldness and faith.

There was a time when my prayers were all about asking God for financial help. I was so focused on my own needs and my own desires that I was not truly seeking His will. But as I grew in my faith, I realised that prayer is not just about asking God for things; it is about aligning our hearts with His. It is about surrendering our own agendas and asking for His will to be done. When I started to pray for God to work in me, not just for me, everything changed. I began to see my business not as a means to my own success, but as a platform for His glory.

I encourage you to make prayer a non-negotiable part of your business routine. Start each day with a prayer of surrender, asking God to guide your steps and to use you for His purposes. When you are faced with a difficult decision, take it to God in prayer. When you are feeling overwhelmed or discouraged, find strength in His presence. When you make God the CEO of your business, you will be amazed at what He can do.

Taking Imperfect Action

One of the biggest obstacles to taking action is the desire for perfection. We wait for the perfect plan, the perfect time, the perfect circumstances. But the truth is that there is no such thing as perfect. Perfection is a myth that keeps us stuck in a state of inaction. If you wait for everything to be perfect before you take action, you will be waiting forever.

The key is to embrace the power of imperfect action. This means being willing to move forward even when you do not have it all figured out. It means being willing to make mistakes, to learn from your failures, and to adjust your course along the way. It means choosing progress over perfection.

When I look back on my own journey, I can see that it was full of imperfect action. I made countless mistakes. I launched products that failed. I hired the wrong people. I wasted time and money on things that did not work. But I also learned from every single one of those experiences. Each failure was a lesson in disguise, a stepping stone on the path to success. If I had waited for everything to be perfect, I would still be waiting.

So, I want to give you permission to be imperfect. I want to give you permission to make mistakes. I want to give you permission to fail. The only true failure is the failure to take action. As long as you are moving forward, as long as you are learning and growing, you are succeeding.

Do not be afraid to put yourself out there, even when you do not feel ready. Launch that website, even if it is not perfect. Write that blog post, even if you are not sure if anyone will read it. Create that product, even if you are not sure if anyone will buy it. The more you take action, the more you will learn, the more you will grow, and the more you will succeed. The journey of a thousand miles, begins with a single step. Take that step today. Take it imperfectly, but take it. Your vision is waiting for you.

Overcoming the Fear of Action

Even with a clear vision and a solid plan, the act of taking action can be terrifying. Fear is often the single greatest obstacle that stands between us and our dreams. It whispers insidious lies in our ears: "What if I fail?" "What if people judge me?" "What if I am not good enough?" This internal monologue of doubt can be so powerful that it paralyses us, preventing us from taking the very steps that would lead to our success.

One of the most common fears is the fear of failure. We live in a society that often stigmatises failure, treating it as a sign of weakness or incompetence. We are taught from a young age to avoid mistakes and to strive for perfection. This creates a deep-seated fear of not measuring up, of falling short of expectations. As entrepreneurs, this fear can be particularly acute. Our businesses are often deeply personal, intertwined with our identities and our sense of self-worth. The thought of our business failing can feel like a personal failure; a public declaration of our inadequacy.

To overcome this fear, we must fundamentally change our

relationship with failure. We must stop seeing it as an endpoint and start seeing it as a vital part of the learning process. Every successful entrepreneur has a long list of failures and setbacks that preceded their success. These experiences were not detours; they were the very path to their eventual triumph. Failure provides invaluable feedback. It shows us what is not working, allowing us to adjust our strategy and try a different approach. It builds resilience, teaching us how to bounce back from adversity and to persevere in the face of challenges. It cultivates humility, reminding us that we do not have all the answers and that we are always learning.

When you reframe failure as a learning opportunity, it loses its power over you. You are no longer afraid to try new things, to take risks, and to step outside of your comfort zone. You understand that even if you do not achieve the desired outcome, you will have gained valuable knowledge and experience that will serve you in the future. As the inventor Thomas Edison famously said: "I have not failed. I've just found 10,000 ways that won't work." This is the mindset of a fearless entrepreneur.

Another pervasive fear is the fear of judgment. We are social creatures, and we have a deep-seated need for approval and acceptance. The thought of being criticised, ridiculed, or rejected can be incredibly painful. This fear can prevent us from sharing our ideas, from putting our work out into the world, and from being our authentic selves. We water down our message, we hide our true personality, and we try to please everyone, all in an attempt to avoid the sting of disapproval.

I remember this fear vividly from my own journey. I was so scared of what people would say, of the potential for mockery or discouragement. I had heard the negative voices before: "You can't do that," "No one in your family has ever done that," "Maybe God doesn't want you to have that." These words echoed in my mind, creating a prison of fear. I put immense pressure on myself to succeed, not for my own fulfilment, but to prove the doubters wrong. This pressure was a heavy burden, one that fuelled my anxiety and stole my joy.

Overcoming the fear of judgment requires a radical shift in focus. You must stop seeking validation from the outside world and start finding it within yourself and in your relationship with God. You must come to a place where you know, deep in your soul, that you are worthy and capable, regardless of what anyone else thinks. Your value is not determined by the opinions of others; it is inherent and God-given. When you truly believe this, the fear of judgment begins to fade. You are no longer performing for an audience; you are living out your purpose with courage and conviction.

It is also important to be selective about whose opinions you allow to influence you. Not everyone deserves a front-row seat in your life. Surround yourself with people who believe in you, who support your dreams, and who will speak life into you, not death. Seek out mentors, coaches, and peers who will challenge you to grow but will also lift you up when you fall. And when the inevitable critics and naysayers appear, learn to see their words for what they often are: a reflection of their own fears and limitations, not a true measure of your potential.

The Discipline of Consistency

Action is not a one-time event; it is a daily discipline. It is the commitment to show up and do the work, day in and day out, even when you do not feel motivated. Motivation is a fickle emotion. It comes and goes like the tide. If you only take action when you feel inspired, you will never achieve the level of success you desire. Discipline, on the other hand, is a choice. It is the decision to do what needs to be done, regardless of how you feel. It is the engine of consistency, and consistency is the key to long-term success.

For busy business mums, consistency can be a huge challenge. We are constantly juggling multiple priorities, and it is easy for our own goals to get pushed to the bottom of the list. We tell ourselves that we will work on our business when we have more time, when the kids are older, or when things are less chaotic. But the truth is that there will never be a perfect time. We must learn to create time and to be disciplined in how we use it.

One of the most effective strategies for building consistency is to create a routine. A routine is a pre-determined sequence of actions that you perform at the same time each day. It takes the guesswork out of your day and reduces the amount of willpower you need to exert. When you have a routine, you do not have to decide what to do next; you simply follow the plan. This frees up your mental energy to focus on the task at hand.

Your morning routine is particularly important. The way you start your day sets the tone for everything that follows. Instead of waking up and immediately checking your phone, which puts you in a reactive state, create a morning routine that is centred around your own well-being and your most important goals. This might include prayer, meditation, journaling, exercise, or reading. It should also include a block of time dedicated to working on your most important business task for the day. By tackling your biggest priority first, you ensure that you are making progress on your goals before the distractions of the day begin to creep in.

Another powerful tool for building consistency is time-blocking. Time-blocking is the practice of scheduling specific blocks of time in your calendar for your most important tasks. Instead of having a to-do list, you have a to-do calendar. This forces you to be realistic about how much you can accomplish in a day, and it helps you to protect your time from the constant interruptions and demands of others. When you have a block of time scheduled for a specific task, you are much more likely to do it.

Remember, the goal is not to be perfect; it is to be consistent. There will be days when your routine gets thrown off, when your kids get sick, or when you simply do not have the energy to do what you planned. That is okay. The key is to not let one bad day turn into a bad week or a bad month. Give yourself grace and get back on track as soon as you can. It is the cumulative effect of your daily actions that will ultimately determine your success.

Taking action is the most challenging, yet most rewarding, part of the entrepreneurial journey. It is where the rubber meets the road, where your vision begins to take shape, and where your dreams start to become a reality. It requires courage, discipline, and a willingness to embrace imperfection. But with each small step you take, you will build momentum, you will gain confidence, and you will move closer to the life of fearless wealth that you were created to live. So, take a deep breath, and take that first step. The world is waiting for you.

CHAPTER 3
STRENGTHEN YOUR LEADERSHIP ROLE

As your business grows, so does your role as a leader. This transition from a solo entrepreneur, or a small business owner, to a leader of a team and a community is one of the most significant and challenging shifts you will make. It requires a new set of skills, a new mindset, and a new level of personal and professional maturity. Leadership is not simply about managing people or delegating tasks, it is about inspiring a shared vision, fostering a culture of trust and collaboration, and empowering others to reach their full potential. For the ambitious business woman, this leadership role extends beyond the workplace and into the home, creating a dual responsibility that is both demanding and deeply rewarding.

Effective leadership is the cornerstone of a sustainable and scalable business. Without it, even the most brilliant vision and the most diligent action will eventually falter. A strong leader provides the direction, the stability, and the motivation that a growing organisation needs to navigate the inevitable challenges and opportunities that come its way. You are the captain of the ship, and your team is looking to you to steer them through calm and stormy seas alike. Your confidence, your clarity, and your courage will set the tone for the entire organisation.

But what does it mean to be a leader, especially as a woman of faith? It is not about adopting a command-and-control style, nor is it about being the loudest voice in the room. True leadership, particularly from a Christian perspective, is rooted in service, humility, and integrity. It is about leading with purpose, inspiring your team through your actions as much as your words, and creating an environment where people feel valued, respected, and empowered. It is about modelling the behaviour you want to see in others, both in your business and in your family.

When you lead with impact, you earn the trust and respect of those around you. Your team will be more engaged, more committed, and more willing to go the extra mile to help you achieve your goals. Your family will feel more secure, more supported, and more connected to your journey. You become living proof that it is possible to build a successful business without sacrificing your values or your relationships. You demonstrate that ambition and compassion can coexist, and that strength and humility are two sides of the same coin. This is the essence of fearless leadership, and it is a skill that you can, and must develop.

The Mindset of a Kingdom Leader

For the Christian business owner, leadership is not just a role; it is a calling. It is an opportunity to reflect the character of Christ in the marketplace and to build a business that is a force for good in the world. This requires a fundamental shift in mindset, a move away from the world's definition of success and towards a kingdom-focused approach to leadership. The Apostle Paul, in his letter to the Philippians, provides a powerful blueprint for this kind of leadership: "Do nothing out of selfish ambition or vain conceit. Rather, in humility value others above yourselves, not looking to your own interests but each of you to the interests of the others. In your relationships with one another, have the same mindset as Christ Jesus" (Philippians 2:3-5).

This passage is a radical departure from the prevailing leadership philosophies of our time, which often emphasise self-promotion, competition, and a relentless focus on the bottom line. A kingdom leader, by contrast, is motivated by a desire to serve, to uplift, and to empower. They are not driven by ego or a need for personal glory, but by a genuine love for people and a deep sense of purpose. They understand that their business is not just a vehicle for personal wealth, but a platform for making a positive impact on the lives of their employees, their customers, and their community.

Adopting the mindset of Christ in your leadership has profound practical implications. It means treating your employees with dignity and respect, not as cogs in a machine, but as valuable individuals created in the image of God. It means creating a culture of grace, where people feel safe to make mistakes, to learn from their failures, and to grow both personally and professionally. It means being generous with your resources, sharing your success with those who have helped you achieve it, and using your profits to make a difference in the world.

It also means leading with integrity, even when it is difficult or costly. It means being honest in your dealings, keeping your promises, and taking responsibility for your actions. In a world where ethical shortcuts are all too common, a leader who operates with unwavering integrity will stand out. Your reputation for honesty and trustworthiness will become one of your greatest assets, attracting loyal customers, dedicated employees, and valuable partners.

One of the most powerful examples of kingdom leadership in the Bible is the story of Deborah in the book of Judges. At a time when Israel was oppressed by the Canaanites, God raised up Deborah, a prophetess and a judge, to lead His people. She was a woman of great wisdom, courage, and faith. She did not lead by force or by title, but by the power of her character and the anointing of God on her life. She inspired the Israelite army, led by Barak, to a miraculous victory over their enemies. Deborah's story is a powerful reminder that God can use anyone, regardless of their gender or their station in life, to be a great leader. It is also a testament to the power of a leader who is fully surrendered to God's will and who leads with wisdom, faith, and a deep love for her people.

As a business mum, you have a unique opportunity to be a Deborah in your own sphere of influence. You can lead with a combination of strength and compassion, of wisdom and grace. You can inspire your team to achieve great things, while also nurturing a culture of care and support. You can build a thriving business, while also raising a strong and healthy family. It is not an easy path, but it is a possible one, and it is the path of a true kingdom leader.

Building a Team That Shares Your Vision

As your business grows, you will reach a point where you can no longer do everything yourself. You will need to build a team to support you and to help you carry the load. This is a critical juncture in the life of any business, and the decisions you make at this stage will have a profound impact on your future success. Hiring the right people is one of the most important things you will ever do as a leader.

It is not enough to hire people who are skilled and experienced.

You must hire people who share your vision and your values. When your team is aligned with your core purpose, you create a powerful synergy that can propel your business to new heights. Everyone is pulling in the same direction, motivated by a shared sense of mission. This creates a culture of collaboration, innovation, and mutual support. When your team is not aligned with your vision, however, you create a culture of conflict, confusion, and inefficiency. You spend your time managing disagreements, resolving disputes, and trying to get everyone on the same page. It is an exhausting and unsustainable way to run a business.

I learned this lesson in the most painful way possible. I once had a manager who I trusted implicitly. She was skilled, experienced, and seemed to be fully committed to the success of the business. But over time, it became clear that her vision was not aligned with mine. She was motivated by her own self-interest, not by the mission of the company. This misalignment culminated in a devastating act of betrayal. While I was away, she attempted to sabotage the company, spreading malicious lies and even redirecting client payments to her own company. It was a shocking and heartbreaking experience, one that nearly destroyed the business I had worked so hard to build.

This painful episode taught me an invaluable lesson about the importance of hiring for character as much as for competence. It is not enough for someone to be good at their job; they must also be a person of integrity, someone who you can trust to act in the best interests of the company, even when you are not watching. Since that experience, I have become much more intentional in my hiring process. I take the time to get to know potential employees on a deeper level. I ask them about their values, their passions, and their long-term goals. I look for people who are not just looking for a job, but who are looking for a mission, people who are excited about the vision of the company and who want to be a part of something bigger than themselves.

Here are some practical steps you can take to build a team that shares your vision:

1. **Define Your Company Culture.** Before you hire anyone, take the time to define the culture you want to create. What are your core values? What kind of work environment do you want to foster? What are the non-negotiable behaviours you expect from your team members? When you are clear about your culture, you can hire people who are a good fit for it.

2. **Hire for Attitude and Train for Skill.** While skills and experience are important, they can often be taught. Attitude, on the other hand, is much more difficult to change. Look for people who are positive, proactive, and passionate. Hire people who are eager to learn, who are not afraid of a challenge, and who have a strong work ethic.

These are the people who will help you build a thriving and resilient business.

3. **Involve Your Team in the Hiring Process.** When you are hiring for a new position, involve your existing team members in the process. They have a vested interest in hiring the right person, and they can often provide valuable insights into a candidate's fit with the company culture. This also sends a powerful message to your team that you value their opinion and trust their judgment.

4. **Communicate Your Vision Constantly.** Do not assume that your team knows what your vision is. You must communicate it constantly, in your words and in your actions. Talk about it in your team meetings. Share stories that illustrate it. Celebrate wins that are in alignment with it. The more you talk about your vision, the more it will become a part of the fabric of your company.

5. **Invest in Your Team's Growth.** When you invest in your team's personal and professional growth, you are sending a powerful message that you care about them as individuals, not just as employees. Provide them with opportunities for training and development. Mentor them. Coach them. Help them to achieve their own personal and professional goals. When you invest in your team, they will invest in you.

Building a team that shares your vision is not a one-time event; it is an ongoing process. It requires intentionality, patience, and a deep commitment to creating a culture of trust and collaboration. But the rewards are immeasurable. A strong and cohesive team is the engine of a successful business, and it is the key to achieving your vision without sacrificing your sanity.

The Art of Delegation

For many entrepreneurs, especially those who are used to doing everything themselves, delegation can be a major challenge. We often fall into the trap of thinking that it is faster and easier to just do it ourselves. We may not trust our team to do the work to our standards, or we may feel guilty about asking others to take on more responsibility. But the inability to delegate is one of the biggest bottlenecks to business growth. It leads to burnout for the leader and disempowerment for the team. If you want to scale your business and create a life of freedom and flexibility, you must master the art of delegation.

Delegation is not just about offloading tasks you do not want to do. It is a strategic tool for leveraging your time and talent, and for developing the skills and confidence of your team. When you delegate effectively, you free yourself up to focus on the high-value activities that only you can do. These are the tasks that require your unique vision, expertise, and leadership. At the same time, you provide your team members with opportunities to learn, to grow, and to take on more ownership in the business. It is a win-win situation.

My own journey with delegation was a rocky one. I was the classic over-functioner, the one who tried to do everything myself. I was working late into the night, taking work home with me, and still feeling like I was constantly behind. I was exhausted, overwhelmed, and on the verge of burnout. My team, on the other hand, was under-utilised and disengaged. They were waiting for me to tell them what to do, and they were not taking the initiative to solve problems or to come up with new ideas. It was a dysfunctional and unsustainable dynamic.

It was not until I hit my breaking point that I realised something had to change. I had to let go of my need for control and start trusting my team. I had to stop being the hero and start being the coach. It was a difficult and scary transition, but it was absolutely essential. I started by delegating small tasks, and as my team proved their competence, I gradually gave them more responsibility. I invested in their training, I coached them, and I created a culture where it was safe to make mistakes. Over time, a remarkable transformation took place. My team became more confident, more proactive, and more committed. And I became more relaxed, more focused, and more effective as a leader.

Here are some key principles for effective delegation:

1. **Delegate Outcomes, Not Tasks.** Instead of telling your team members exactly how to do something, tell them what you want to achieve. Give them a clear picture of the desired outcome, and then give them the freedom to figure out the best way to get there. This fosters a sense of ownership and encourages creativity and innovation.

2. **Provide Clear Instructions and Expectations.** While you do not want to micromanage, you do need to provide your team with the information they need to succeed. Be clear about the scope of the project, the deadline, the budget, and any other relevant parameters. Make sure they understand what success looks like, and how their work will be evaluated.

3. **Give Them the Authority They Need.** You cannot delegate responsibility without also delegating authority. Your team members need to have the authority to make decisions, to access resources, and to take action without having to come to you for approval at every turn. This is a crucial element of empowerment.

4. **Create a Safe Environment for Failure.** If you want your team to take risks and to be innovative, you must create an environment where it is safe to fail. When someone makes a mistake, do not punish them. Instead, use it as a learning

opportunity. Help them to understand what went wrong and how they can do better next time. This will build their confidence and their resilience.

5. **Provide Feedback and Recognition.** Regular feedback is essential for growth. Let your team members know what they are doing well and where they can improve. Be specific, constructive, and timely in your feedback. And do not forget to recognise and celebrate their successes. A little bit of appreciation can go a long way in boosting morale and motivation.

Delegation is a skill that takes time and practice to develop. It requires a shift in mindset from being a doer to being a leader. But it is a skill that is absolutely essential for building a scalable and sustainable business. When you learn to delegate effectively, you will not only achieve more, but you will also create a more empowered and engaged team, and a more balanced and fulfilling life for yourself.

Leading at Home

For the business mum, leadership does not stop at the office door. It extends into the home, where you are the co-leader of your family. The same principles of vision, communication, and empowerment that apply in your business also apply in your family. In fact, your leadership at home is arguably even more important, as it is shaping the lives and the futures of your children.

One of the greatest challenges for any working mother is the constant tension between work and family. We are often pulled in a million different directions, and it is easy to feel like we are not doing a good enough job in either role. We feel guilty when we are at work, and we feel guilty when we are at home. It is a relentless cycle of self-recrimination.

But it does not have to be this way. When you lead with intentionality and purpose, you can create a family life that is not only compatible with your business ambitions, but that is also enriched by them. Your children can learn valuable lessons from watching you build a business. They can learn about hard work, resilience, and the importance of pursuing your dreams. You can model for them what it looks like to be a strong, confident, and compassionate leader.

Here are some strategies for leading effectively at home:

1. **Create a Family Vision.** Just as you have a vision for your business, you should also have a vision for your family. What are your family's core values? What kind of family culture do you want to create? What are your shared goals and dreams? When you have a clear family vision, it can guide your decisions and help you to stay united, even when things get tough.

2. **Communicate Openly and Honestly.** Communication is the lifeblood of any healthy family. Create a safe space where everyone feels comfortable sharing their thoughts, their feelings, and their needs. Listen to your children without judgment, and validate their emotions. Be honest with them about your own struggles and your own triumphs. When you are open and vulnerable with your children, you build a foundation of trust that will last a lifetime.

3. **Empower Your Children.** Just as you empower your team at work, you should also empower your children at home. Give them age-appropriate responsibilities, and let them experience the natural consequences of their choices. Teach them how to solve their own problems, and resist the urge to rescue them from every struggle. When you empower your children, you are giving them the gift of self-confidence and resilience.

4. **Be Present.** In our hyper-connected world, it is easy to be physically present but mentally absent. When you are with your children, make a conscious effort to be fully present. Put away your phone, turn off the television, and give them your undivided attention. Listen to their stories, play their games, and enter into their world. These moments of connection are the building blocks of a strong and healthy relationship.

5. **Prioritise Your Marriage.** If you are married, your relationship with your spouse is the foundation of your family. It is the source of your strength, your support, and your sanity. You must make it a priority to nurture that relationship. Schedule regular date nights, communicate openly and honestly, and work together as a team. When your marriage is strong, your entire family will be stronger.

Leading at home is not about being a perfect mother. It is about being an intentional one. It is about creating a family culture that is based on love, respect, and mutual support. It is about raising children who are confident, resilient, and compassionate. And it is about building a life that is not just successful, but also deeply meaningful. As a business mum, you have the unique opportunity to be a powerful leader in both your business and your home. It is a high ministry, but it is one that you are more than capable of fulfilling.

The Leader's Self-Care

In the midst of leading a team and a family, it is easy for a business woman to neglect the most important person in her life: herself. We are so focused on taking care of everyone else that we often put our own needs last. We sacrifice sleep, we skip meals, and we ignore the warning signs of burnout, all in the name of being a good leader and a good mother. But this is an unhealthy and unsustainable way to live. You cannot pour from an empty cup. If you do not take care of yourself, you will eventually have nothing left to give to your business or your family.

Self-care is not a luxury; it is a necessity. It is the fuel that allows you to show up as the best version of yourself, both personally and professionally. When you are well-rested, well-nourished, and emotionally balanced, you are more creative, more resilient, and more effective as a leader. You are better able to handle stress, to make good decisions, and to inspire those around you. When you are depleted, on the other hand, you are more likely to be irritable, reactive, and overwhelmed. You are more likely to make mistakes, to damage relationships, and to burn out.

For many women, especially those who are high-achievers, self-care can feel selfish. We have been conditioned to believe that our value comes from what we do for others, and that taking time for ourselves is a sign of weakness or indulgence. But this is a lie. The truth is that self-care is one of the most selfless things you can do. When you take care of yourself, you are ensuring that you have the energy, the patience, and the capacity to take care of those who depend on you. You are giving them the gift of a healthy, happy, and whole you.

So, what does self-care look like for a busy business woman? It is not about grand gestures or expensive spa days, although those can be nice too. It is about building small, sustainable habits into your daily life that nourish your body, your mind, and your soul. It is about making a conscious and consistent effort to prioritise your own well-being.

Here are some practical self-care strategies you can implement:

1. **Protect Your Sleep.** Sleep is not a luxury; it is a biological necessity. When you are sleep-deprived, your cognitive function, your emotional regulation, and your physical health all suffer. Aim for 7-9 hours of quality sleep per night. Create a relaxing bedtime routine, and make your bedroom a sanctuary for sleep. Avoid caffeine and alcohol before bed, and turn off all screens at least an hour before you go to sleep.
2. **Nourish Your Body.** The food you eat has a direct impact on your energy levels, your mood, and your overall health. Fuel your body with whole, nutrient-dense foods. Avoid processed foods, sugary drinks, and excessive amounts of caffeine. Drink plenty of water throughout the day. And do not skip meals, no matter how busy you are. Your body needs a consistent supply of energy to function at its best.
3. **Move Your Body.** Exercise is one of the most powerful tools for reducing stress, boosting your mood, and increasing your energy levels. Find a form of movement that you enjoy, and make it a regular part of your routine. It does not have to be a high-intensity workout at the gym. A brisk walk in nature, a yoga class, or a dance party in your

living room can all be effective forms of exercise. The key is to be consistent.

4. **Nurture Your Soul.** As a woman of faith, your spiritual health is just as important as your physical and mental health. Make time for prayer, meditation, and reading the Bible. Connect with a community of believers who can support you and encourage you in your faith. And remember to spend time in nature, where you can experience the beauty and the majesty of God's creation.

5. **Schedule "Me Time."** In addition to your daily self-care habits, it is also important to schedule regular blocks of time for activities that you enjoy, just for the sake of enjoyment. This could be anything from reading a book, to taking a bath, to having coffee with a friend. The key is to do something that fills you up and that has no other purpose than to bring you joy. Protect this time in your calendar as fiercely as you would protect a meeting with your most important client.

Being a leader is a marathon, not a sprint. It requires stamina, resilience, and a deep well of personal resources. Self-care is what fills that well. It is what allows you to lead with strength, with grace, and with joy. It is what enables you to build a business and a life that you love, without sacrificing yourself in the process. So, I urge you, do not neglect this crucial aspect of your leadership journey. Make self-care a non-negotiable priority. Your business, your family, and your future self will thank you for it.

CHAPTER 4
UPLIFT YOURSELF WITH POSITIVITY

The journey of an entrepreneur, especially a business woman, is a rollercoaster of emotions. There are exhilarating highs, crushing lows, and long stretches of uncertainty in between. In the midst of this volatility, your mindset is not just a contributing factor to your success; it is the very foundation upon which it is built. A positive and resilient mindset is the invisible force that will carry you through the challenges, empower you to see opportunities in the midst of adversity, and ultimately determine whether you thrive or merely survive. It is the difference between being a victim of your circumstances and being the victorious creator of your life.

Positivity is not about ignoring the realities of your situation or pretending that everything is perfect when it is not. That is denial, and it is a toxic and unproductive state of mind. True positivity, especially from a faith-based perspective, is an active and courageous choice. It is the decision to focus on solutions rather than problems, on possibilities rather than limitations, and on God's promises rather than your fears. It is a Christ-like mindset that acknowledges the challenges but refuses to be defined by them. It is the unwavering belief that with God, all things are possible, and that He can turn any situation around for your good.

Your thoughts are incredibly powerful. They shape your emotions, your actions, and ultimately, your destiny. The Bible tells us in Proverbs 23:7, "As a man thinks in his heart, so is he." If you constantly dwell on thoughts of fear, doubt, and negativity, you will create a life that is characterised by those very things. You will be timid in your actions, hesitant in your decisions, and you will attract more of the circumstances you are trying to avoid. If, on the other hand, you cultivate a mindset of faith, hope, and positivity, you will create a life that is filled with courage, resilience, and abundance. You will approach challenges with confidence, you will see opportunities where others see obstacles, and you will attract the people and the resources you need to succeed.

This is not just wishful thinking; it is a spiritual and psychological principle. The words you speak and the thoughts you entertain create an atmosphere around you. They are like seeds that you are constantly planting in the garden of your life. If you plant seeds of negativity, you will reap a harvest of weeds and thorns. If you plant seeds of positivity, you will reap a harvest of fruit and flowers. As it says in Proverbs 18:21, "Death and life are in the power of the tongue, and those who love it will eat its fruits." You have the power to speak life into your business, your family, and your future. The question is, what kind of life are you speaking?

I have experienced the transformative power of this principle in my own life. There was a time when I was consumed by fear and negativity. The loss of a major contract, the betrayal of a trusted employee, and the immense pressure of juggling my business and my family had left me in a dark and hopeless place. My thoughts were a constant barrage of "what ifs" and "I can'ts." I was convinced that I was going to lose everything I had worked so hard for. And as long as I remained in that negative mindset, my reality reflected it. I was stuck, paralysed by fear, and unable to see a way forward.

It was only when I made a conscious decision to change my thinking that things began to shift. I started to intentionally replace my negative thoughts with positive ones. I began to declare God's promises over my life and my business. I started to focus on what I could do, instead of what I could not. It was not an easy or an overnight process, but with each small step I took towards a more positive mindset, I felt a little bit stronger, a little bit more hopeful, and a little bit more empowered. And as my mindset changed, so did my circumstances. I began to see solutions where I had only seen problems. I began to attract new opportunities. And slowly but surely, I began to rebuild my business and my life, stronger and more resilient than before. This experience taught me that your mindset is not something that happens to you; it is something that you create. And it is the most powerful tool you have for shaping your reality.

The Science of Positivity

While the concept of a positive mindset has deep spiritual roots, it is also supported by a growing body of scientific research. Neuroscientists have discovered that our brains are not fixed, but are constantly being shaped by our thoughts and experiences. This phenomenon, known as neuroplasticity, means that we have the ability to literally rewire our brains for more positivity, happiness, and success.

When you repeatedly focus on negative thoughts and emotions, you strengthen the neural pathways in your brain that are associated with those states. This makes it easier for you to slip into negativity in the future. It is like creating a well-worn path in a forest. The more you walk down that path, the easier it becomes to follow. In the same way, the more you dwell on negative thoughts, the more you train your brain to be negative.

Conversely, when you intentionally focus on positive thoughts and emotions, you strengthen the neural pathways that are associated with those states. You begin to carve out new paths in your brain, paths of hope, optimism, and resilience. The more you practice positive thinking, the more it becomes your default state. You are literally changing the structure of your brain to support a more positive and empowered way of being.

One of the most powerful ways to do this is through the practice of gratitude. Gratitude is more than just saying thank you; it is a deep sense of appreciation for the good things in your life, both big and small. When you regularly practice gratitude, you shift your focus from what is wrong in your life to what is right. This simple act has a profound impact on your brain and your well-being. Research has shown that gratitude can increase happiness, reduce depression, improve sleep, and even strengthen your immune system.

As a busy business mum, it can be easy to get caught up in the never-ending to-do lists and the constant demands on your time and energy. It is easy to lose sight of the blessings that are all around you. This is why it is so important to make gratitude a daily practice. You can start a gratitude journal, where you write down three to five things you are grateful for each day. You can share what you are grateful for with your family around the dinner table. You can simply take a few moments throughout the day to pause and notice the good things in your life. For example the smile on your child's face, the support of your spouse or the loyalty of your customers.

The practice of gratitude was a lifeline for me during the most difficult period of my life. When our boiler broke and we could not afford to replace it, I had to heat water with a kettle to bathe my children in a bucket. When our cooker failed, I had to improvise and cook meals for my family using only a rice cooker. It would have been easy to despair, to focus on what we lacked. But even in those challenging circumstances, I chose to find things to be grateful for. I was grateful for the resilience of my children, who found joy even in the simplest of meals. I was grateful for my own creativity and resourcefulness. And most of all, I was grateful for the presence of God, who I knew was with me in the midst of the struggle. This practice of gratitude did not change my circumstances overnight, but it changed my perspective. It gave me the strength to persevere, and it reminded me that even in the darkest of times, there is always something to be thankful for.

The Power of Affirmations

Another powerful tool for rewiring your brain for positivity is the use of affirmations. Affirmations are positive statements that you repeat to yourself on a regular basis. They are designed to challenge and overcome self-sabotaging and negative thoughts. When you repeat an affirmation over and over again, it begins to sink into your subconscious mind, and it starts to change the way you think, feel, and behave.

For many people, the idea of affirmations can feel a bit strange or even silly at first. But the truth is that we are all using affirmations all the time, whether we realise it or not. The thoughts that you repeat to yourself on a daily basis are a form of affirmation. If you are constantly telling yourself, "I am not good enough," "I can't do this," or "I am going to fail," you are affirming a negative reality for yourself. The goal of positive affirmations is to intentionally choose the messages that you are sending to your subconscious mind.

To be effective, affirmations should be stated in the present tense, as if they are already true. They should be positive, personal, and specific. For example, instead of saying, "I will be a successful business owner," you would say, "I am a successful and prosperous business owner." Instead of saying, "I will not be afraid," you would say, "I am courageous and confident."

Here are some examples of powerful affirmations for a business woman:

- I am a capable, resilient, and visionary leader.
- I rise above fear and choose faith.
- I can do all things through Christ who strengthens me.
- I am a loving and present mother and a successful and passionate business owner.

- I attract abundance and prosperity into my life and my business.
- I am worthy of success and happiness.
- I am creating a life that honours God, a life that is aligned with His Word, my deepest values, and the calling He has placed on my heart.

I recommend creating a list of 10-15 affirmations that resonate with you and that address the specific areas where you want to see a change in your mindset. You can write them down on index cards and place them where you will see them throughout the day; on your bathroom mirror, on your computer monitor, or on the dashboard of your car. You can also record yourself saying them and listen to them while you are driving or getting ready in the morning. The key is to repeat them consistently, with feeling and with conviction.

When you first start using affirmations, you may experience some internal resistance. Your conscious mind may argue with the positive statements, reminding you of all the evidence to the contrary. This is normal. It is a sign that the affirmations are challenging your old, limiting beliefs. Do not be discouraged. Keep repeating the affirmations, and over time, they will begin to override the negative programming in your subconscious mind. You will start to believe them, and as you believe them, you will start to act in accordance with them. And as you act in accordance with them, you will start to see them manifest in your life.

A Christ-Like Mindset

For the Christian business woman, the pursuit of positivity is not just about self-improvement; it is about cultivating a Christ-like mindset. It is about learning to see the world, ourselves, and our circumstances through the lens of faith. A Christ-like mindset is not one that denies the existence of problems; it is one that focuses on the problem-solver. It is a mindset that is rooted in the unwavering belief that God is good, that He is in control, and that He can work all things together for our good.

One of the key characteristics of a Christ-like mindset is a focus on solutions rather than problems. When we are faced with a challenge, it is easy to get bogged down in the details of the problem. We can spend hours, days, or even weeks analysing what went wrong, who is to blame, and how terrible the situation is. But this is a fruitless and disempowering exercise. A Christ-like mindset, on the other hand, acknowledges the problem and then immediately shifts its focus to finding a solution. It asks, "What can I learn from this?" "What is the opportunity in this challenge?" "What is the next right step I can take?"

This solution-focused mindset is a game-changer for any entrepreneur. It transforms you from a passive victim into an active problem-solver. It empowers you to take control of your circumstances and to create the outcomes you desire. It also builds your resilience, as you begin to see challenges not as roadblocks, but as stepping stones on the path to success.

Another key aspect of a Christ-like mindset is a commitment to speaking life into every situation. As we have already discussed, our words have the power to create our reality. When we speak words of doubt, fear, and negativity, we are partnering with the enemy and giving him a foothold in our lives. When we speak words of faith, hope, and encouragement, we are partnering with God and releasing His power into our circumstances. This is why it is so important to be intentional about the words we speak, both to ourselves and to others. We must learn to be our own biggest cheerleaders, to encourage ourselves in the Lord, and to speak life into our businesses, our families, and our futures.

I had to learn this lesson in the midst of my greatest trial. When my business was on the verge of collapse, it would have been easy to speak words of defeat and despair. But I made a conscious choice to speak words of faith and hope instead. I declared that my business would not fail, that God would provide, and that I would come out of this stronger than before. I spoke life into my team, into my clients, and into my own heart. And as I did, I felt a shift in the atmosphere. Hope began to replace despair, and faith began to replace fear. My words were not just a reflection of my reality; they were a creative force that was shaping my reality.

Finally, a Christ-like mindset is one that is rooted in a deep and abiding trust in God's sovereignty. It is the unwavering belief that God is in control, even when our circumstances seem to be out of control. It is the confidence that He has a plan for our lives, and that His plan is good. This trust is not a passive resignation to fate; it is an active and courageous choice to place our hope in God, rather than in our own abilities or in the stability of our circumstances. It is the anchor that holds us steady in the midst of the storms of life.

During the most difficult season of my entrepreneurial journey, my faith was tested to its limits. I was facing financial ruin, betrayal, and the overwhelming stress of trying to hold my business and my family together. There were many moments when I felt like I was drowning. But in the midst of it all, I clung to my faith. I remembered the story of Ezekiel, how God commanded the dry bones to come alive, and they did. I believed that if God could bring hope to a valley of dry bones, He could surely bring hope to my seemingly hopeless situation. This trust in God's sovereignty did not make my problems disappear, but it gave me the strength to face them. It gave me a peace that surpassed all understanding. And it gave me the unwavering conviction that no matter what happened, God was with me, and He would never leave me nor forsake me.

Cultivating a positive and Christ-like mindset is not a one-time decision; it is a daily practice. It requires intentionality, discipline, and a deep reliance on the grace of God. But it is a practice that will transform your life and your business. It will empower you to overcome challenges, to seize opportunities, and to build a life of fearless wealth and abundant joy. So, I encourage you, choose positivity. Choose faith. Choose to see yourself and your circumstances through the eyes of God. And watch as your world begins to change.

The Danger of the Comparison Trap

In our hyper-connected, social media-driven world, it has never been easier to fall into the comparison trap. With a few clicks, we can get a curated glimpse into the seemingly perfect lives and businesses of others. We see the highlight reels; the product launches, the client testimonials, the family holidays and we inevitably compare them to our own behind-the-scenes reality, which is often messy, chaotic, and full of challenges. This constant comparison is a recipe for discontent, envy, and self-doubt. It is one of the most effective joy-stealers and motivation-killers for any entrepreneur.

When we compare ourselves to others, we are playing a game we can never win. There will always be someone who seems to be more successful, more talented, or more put-together than we are. We are comparing our Chapter 1 to someone else's Chapter 20. We are not seeing the years of hard work, the countless failures, and the immense sacrifices that went into creating their success. We are only seeing the polished final product. This creates an unrealistic and unfair standard for ourselves, and it can leave us feeling inadequate and discouraged.

The comparison trap is particularly tough for women, who are often socialised to be more attuned to the opinions and achievements of others. We can get so caught up in what everyone else is doing that we lose sight of our own unique path and our own unique calling. We start to believe that there is only one right way to build a business, and that if we are not following that formula, we are doing something wrong. This can stifle our creativity, our innovation, and our authenticity.

So, how do we escape the comparison trap? It starts with a conscious decision to focus on our own journey. We must learn to put on our blinders and to run our own race. This does not mean that we cannot learn from others or be inspired by their success. But it does mean that we must stop using their journey as a measuring stick for our own. Our journey is unique, our calling is unique, and our definition of success is unique. The only person we should be comparing ourselves to is the person we were yesterday.

Here are some practical strategies for overcoming the comparison trap:

1. **Curate Your Social Media Feed.** You have control over the content that you consume. Unfollow any accounts that leave you feeling inadequate or discouraged. Follow accounts that inspire you, that educate you, and that make you feel good about yourself. Be intentional about creating a social media environment that is positive and uplifting.

2. **Practice Gratitude.** As we have already discussed, gratitude is a powerful antidote to comparison. When you are focused on what you are grateful for in your own life, you are less likely to be envious of what others have. Make gratitude a daily practice, and watch as your perspective begins to shift.

3. **Celebrate Your Own Progress.** Instead of focusing on how far you have to go, take the time to celebrate how far you have come. Keep a "win jar" where you write down your accomplishments, both big and small. When you are feeling discouraged, you can pull out the jar and remind yourself of all the progress you have made. This will help you to stay motivated and to appreciate your own unique journey.

4. **Remember Your "Why."** When you are feeling tempted to compare yourself to others, reconnect with your "Big

Why." Remind yourself of the unique purpose and passion that drives you. Your "Why" is your Divine Anchor, and it will keep you focused on your own path, regardless of what anyone else is doing.

5. **Collaborate, Don't Compete.** Instead of seeing other women in your field as your competition, see them as your potential collaborators. Reach out to them, build relationships with them, and look for ways to support each other. When we adopt a mindset of collaboration over competition, we create a powerful community of support that can lift all of us up.

Dealing with Negative People

Just as it is important to curate your social media feed, it is also important to curate your social circle. The people you surround yourself with have a profound impact on your mindset, your energy, and your success. The Bible tells us in 1 Corinthians 15:33, "Do not be deceived: 'Bad company ruins good morals.'" The same is true for our mindset. If you surround yourself with negative, cynical, and discouraging people, it will be incredibly difficult to maintain a positive and empowered mindset.

Negative people, often referred to as "dream stealers," can be found everywhere. They are the ones who will tell you all the reasons why your business idea will not work. They are the ones who will question your abilities and your qualifications. They are the ones who will remind you of all the risks and the potential for failure. They may be well-meaning, but their negativity can be toxic. It can plant seeds of doubt in your mind and can drain you of the energy and the enthusiasm you need to pursue your dreams.

As a leader, you must be ruthless in protecting your energy and your mindset. This means being willing to set boundaries with negative people, or even to remove them from your life altogether. This can be a difficult and painful process, especially if the negative people are close friends or family members. But it is absolutely essential for your well-being and your success.

Here are some strategies for dealing with negative people:

1. **Limit Your Exposure.** If you cannot remove a negative person from your life completely, you can limit your exposure to them. Spend less time with them, and when you are with them, keep the conversation light and avoid topics that are likely to trigger their negativity.

2. **Set Clear Boundaries.** Be clear and direct with negative people about what you will and will not tolerate. You can say something like, "I appreciate your concern, but I am not looking for feedback on my business right now. I would love it if you could just support me and encourage me." If they are not able to respect your boundaries, you may need to distance yourself from them further.

3. **Don't Take It Personally.** Remember that a negative person's negativity is not about you; it is about them. It is a reflection of their own fears, their own insecurities, and their own limiting beliefs. Do not allow their negativity to become your own. See it for what it is, and let it go.

4. **Surround Yourself with Positive People.** The best way to counteract the influence of negative people is to surround yourself with positive, supportive, and encouraging people. Seek out mentors, coaches, and peers who believe in you and who will cheer you on. Create a "mastermind" group of like-minded entrepreneurs who can provide you with support, accountability, and inspiration. When you are surrounded by positivity, the negativity of others will have less of an impact on you.

Your mindset is your most valuable asset. You must protect it fiercely. Be intentional about the content you consume, the people you associate with, and the thoughts you entertain. When you create an environment that is conducive to positivity, you set yourself up for success, not just in your business, but in every area of your life.

The Ripple Effect of Positivity

As a leader, your mindset does not just affect you; it has a ripple effect that extends to your team, your customers, and your family. Your energy is contagious. If you are positive, optimistic, and enthusiastic, you will inspire those around you to be the same. If you are negative, pessimistic, and discouraged, you will drag everyone down with you. This is a tremendous responsibility, but it is also a tremendous opportunity.

When you lead with positivity, you create a culture of optimism and resilience. Your team will be more engaged, more creative, and more willing to go the extra mile. They will be more likely to see challenges as opportunities, and to work together to find innovative solutions. A positive work environment is also a more enjoyable and a more productive one. People are happier, healthier, and more committed when they are working in a culture of positivity.

Your positivity also has a profound impact on your customers. People are drawn to positive and enthusiastic people. When you interact with your customers from a place of genuine positivity, you create a connection that goes beyond the transactional. You build trust, you foster loyalty, and you create raving fans who will not only buy from you, but who will also become your most powerful advocates.

And of course, your mindset has a huge impact on your family. As a mother, you are the emotional thermostat of your home. If you are stressed, anxious, and negative, your children will feel it. If you are calm, happy, and positive, you will create a home environment that is a haven of peace and joy. Your children will learn from your example how to navigate the challenges of life with grace and with resilience. You are not just building a business; you are shaping the next generation of leaders.

The journey of a woman entrepreneur is not an easy one. It is filled with challenges, setbacks, and moments of doubt. But it is also filled with opportunities for growth, for impact, and for joy. The key to navigating this journey successfully is to cultivate a positive and Christ-like mindset. It is the unwavering belief that you are capable, that you are worthy, and that you are destined for greatness. It is the courageous choice to focus on faith over fear, on solutions over problems, and on possibilities over limitations. It is the daily practice of gratitude, of affirmation, and of speaking life into your circumstances. When you master your mindset, you will unlock your full potential. You will become the fearless, prosperous, and joyful woman you were created to be.

Chapter 5

Create Time for Enjoyment

In the relentless pursuit of building a successful business and raising a family, it is incredibly easy for the ambitious business leader to lose sight of a crucial, yet often neglected, element of a fulfilling life: enjoyment. We become so consumed by our to-do lists, our deadlines, and our responsibilities that we forget to make time for the very things that bring us joy, that replenish our souls, and that make the journey worthwhile. We operate under the false assumption that enjoyment is a luxury, a reward to be earned only after we have achieved all of our goals. But this is a dangerous and unsustainable way to live. It is a fast track to burnout, resentment, and a life that, despite its outward success, feels empty and devoid of meaning.

Enjoyment is not a frivolous indulgence; it is an essential component of a healthy and balanced life. It is the secret ingredient that fuels your creativity, that strengthens your relationships, and that gives you the energy and the motivation to persevere through the inevitable challenges of entrepreneurship. When you make time for enjoyment, you are not being selfish; you are being strategic. You are investing in your most valuable asset: yourself. You are refilling your well, so that you have more to give to your business, your family, and your community.

For many high-achieving women, the concept of making time for enjoyment can feel counterintuitive. We are conditioned to believe that our value lies in our productivity, and that any time not spent working or taking care of others is time wasted. We wear our busyness as a badge of honour, and we feel guilty when we take a moment to rest or to do something purely for the pleasure of it. But this mindset is a trap. It leads to a life of constant striving, where the finish line is always just out of reach. It creates a cycle of stress and exhaustion that ultimately undermines our ability to be effective in any area of our lives.

The truth is that you cannot pour from an empty cup. If you are constantly giving to others without taking the time to replenish your own energy, you will eventually have nothing left to give. You will become irritable, resentful, and disengaged. Your work will suffer, your relationships will suffer, and your health will suffer. This is not the life that God has called you to live. He has called you to a life of abundance, a life of joy, and a life of peace. But it is up to you to create the space for that life to unfold.

This was a lesson that I had to learn through painful experience.

There was a time when I was so focused on growing my business that I had no time for anything else. I was working around the clock, sacrificing my sleep, my health, and my relationships. I told myself that it was just for a season, that once I reached a certain level of success, I would be able to relax and enjoy my life. But that day never seemed to come. The more I achieved, the more I had to do. I was trapped on a hamster wheel of my own making, and I was running myself into the ground.

It was not until I hit a wall of complete and utter exhaustion that I realised something had to change. I was successful by all outward measures, but I was miserable. I had lost my joy, my passion, and my sense of purpose. I was a shell of my former self. It was in that moment of crisis that I finally understood the importance of making time for enjoyment. I realised that a life without joy is not a life at all. And so, I began the slow and intentional process of reclaiming my life. I started to schedule time for the things that brought me joy, just as I would schedule a business meeting. I started to set boundaries around my work, and I started to prioritise my own well-being. It was not an easy transition, but it was a life-changing one. And as I began to fill my own cup, I found that I had more to give to my business, my family, and my faith than ever before.

The Biblical Case for Rest and Enjoyment

For the Christian business mum, the idea of making time for enjoyment is not just a good idea; it is a biblical mandate. From the very beginning of creation, God modelled a rhythm of work and rest. After six days of creating the heavens and the earth, He rested on the seventh day. This was not because He was tired; it was because He was establishing a principle for all of humanity to follow. Rest is not a sign of weakness; it is an act of obedience. It is a declaration of our trust in God's provision, and it is an acknowledgment that we are not the source of our own strength.

The concept of Sabbath, a day of rest and worship, is a cornerstone of the Judeo-Christian tradition. It is a weekly reminder that our value is not determined by our productivity, and that we are more than just what we do. It is a time to cease from our striving, to reconnect with God, and to enjoy the fruits of our labour. In a world that is constantly telling us to do more, to be more, and to have more, the practice of Sabbath is a radical act of defiance. It is a declaration that we are choosing to live by a different set of values, the values of the kingdom of God.

But the Bible's call to enjoyment extends beyond the practice of Sabbath. The book of Ecclesiastes, for example, is filled with admonitions to enjoy the simple pleasures of life. "I know that there is nothing better for people than to be happy and to do good while they live. That each of them may eat and drink, and find satisfaction in all their toil—this is the gift of God" (Ecclesiastes 3:12-13). This is a powerful reminder that joy is not something to be postponed until the afterlife; it is a gift to be experienced here and now. God wants us to enjoy the lives He has given us, to find satisfaction in our work, and to delight in the good things He has provided.

One of the most beautiful and comprehensive pictures of a balanced and enjoyable life is found in the description of the Proverbs 31 woman. This woman is often held up as the ideal of a virtuous and industrious wife and mother, and for good reason. She is a savvy businesswoman, a wise manager of her household, and a compassionate caregiver to the poor. But she is not a workaholic. She is also a woman who enjoys the fruits of her labour. "She is clothed with strength and dignity; she can laugh at the days to come" (Proverbs 31:25). This is a woman who is not driven by fear or anxiety, but who is able to live with a sense of joy and confidence. She has created a life that is not only productive, but also deeply satisfying.

The example of the Proverbs 31 woman is a powerful antidote to the modern-day myth of the "superwoman," the woman who tries to do it all and to be it all, often at the expense of her own well-being. The Proverbs 31 woman is not a superwoman; she is a wise woman. She understands the importance of balance, of diligence, and of enjoying the life that God has given her. She is a model for all of us who are striving to build a successful business while also creating a life of meaning, purpose, and joy.

Redefining Enjoyment

When we think of enjoyment, we often think of big, extravagant experiences, exotic holidays, expensive shopping sprees, or lavish parties. And while these things can certainly be enjoyable, they are not the only, or even the most important, sources of joy in our lives. True and lasting joy is often found in the small, simple, and everyday moments. It is found in the laughter of our children, in a quiet cup of coffee before the house wakes up, in a walk in nature, or in a heartfelt conversation with a friend.

As a busy business person, it is essential to redefine your understanding of enjoyment. You must let go of the idea that you need to have large blocks of free time or a lot of extra money to experience joy. Instead, you must learn to find joy in the cracks and crevices of your busy life. You must learn to be present to the small moments of beauty, of connection, and of grace that are all around you.

Here are some practical ways to redefine enjoyment and to incorporate more of it into your daily life:

1. **Practice Stillness.** Stillness is the practice of paying attention to the present moment, without judgment. It is about noticing the sights, the sounds, the smells, and the sensations of your current experience. When you practice

stillness, you are able to step out of the constant stream of thoughts about the past and the future, and to fully inhabit the present moment. This is where joy is found. You can practice stillness while you are drinking your morning coffee, while you are playing with your children, or even while you are washing the dishes. The key is to bring your full attention to the task at hand, and to notice the small details that you might otherwise miss.

2. **Create a "Joy List."** Take some time to brainstorm a list of all the things that bring you joy, both big and small. Do not censor yourself. Write down anything and everything that comes to mind. Your list might include things like reading a novel, taking a bubble bath, listening to your favourite music, gardening, or trying a new recipe. Keep this list somewhere you can see it, and when you have a few spare moments, choose something from the list to do.

3. **Schedule "Micro-Joys."** You may not have time for a two-week holiday, but you probably have time for a five-minute dance party in your kitchen. You may not have time for a full day at the spa, but you probably have time to apply a face mask while you are answering emails. Look for small ways to inject moments of joy into your day. These "micro-joys" can have a surprisingly big impact on your overall sense of well-being.

4. **Connect with Nature.** Spending time in nature is one of the most effective ways to reduce stress, to boost your mood, and to reconnect with a sense of wonder and awe. You do not have to go on a long hike in the wilderness. You can simply take a few moments to sit in your garden, to walk barefoot on the grass, or to look up at the stars. Nature has a way of putting our problems into perspective and of reminding us of the beauty and the majesty of God's creation.

5. **Cultivate a Spirit of Play.** As adults, we often forget how to play. We become so serious and so focused on our responsibilities that we lose our sense of spontaneity and fun. But play is not just for children; it is an essential part of a healthy and joyful life for people of all ages. Make time for activities that have no other purpose than to be fun. Be silly with your children. Have a games night with your family. Try a new hobby. When you give yourself permission to play, you tap into a source of creativity, of connection, and of pure, unadulterated joy.

Making Time for Your Faith

For the Kingdom focussed entrepreneur, one of the most important sources of enjoyment and replenishment is a deep and abiding connection with God. When we are rooted in His presence, we are able to experience a peace that surpasses all understanding, a joy that is not dependent on our circumstances, and a strength that is not our own. But in the hustle and bustle of our busy lives, it is easy for our relationship with God to get pushed to the back burner. We can become so consumed by the demands of our businesses and our families that we neglect the very source of our life and our strength.

This is a dangerous place to be. When we are disconnected from God, we are more susceptible to fear, to anxiety, and to burnout. We are more likely to make decisions based on our own limited understanding, rather than on His infinite wisdom. And we are more likely to lose sight of our true purpose and our ultimate calling. This is why it is so essential to be intentional about making time for your faith, not as another item on your to-do list, but as the very foundation upon which your entire life is built.

I have learned this lesson through my own struggles. There have been times in my life when I have been so busy that I have let my spiritual disciplines slide. I have skipped my morning quiet time, I have rushed through my prayers, and I have gone weeks without opening my Bible. And every single time, the result has been the same: I have become more stressed, more anxious, and more overwhelmed. It is in those moments that I am reminded that I cannot do this life on my own. I need God. I need His wisdom, His strength, and His grace. And the only way to access those things is to spend time in His presence.

Here are some practical ways to make time for your faith, even in the midst of a busy life:

1. **Start Your Day with God.** Before you do anything else, before you check your phone, before you look at your to-do list, take a few moments to connect with God. You can read a short devotional, you can pray, or you can simply sit in silence and listen for His voice. Starting your day with God will help to set the tone for everything that follows. It will remind you of who you are and whose you are, and it will give you the strength and the wisdom you need to face the day.

2. **Incorporate Prayer into Your Daily Routine.** You do not have to set aside an hour for prayer every day. You can incorporate prayer into the activities you are already doing. You can pray while you are driving, while you are washing the dishes, or while you are taking a shower. You can turn your worries into prayers, and you can turn your gratitude into praise. The key is to cultivate a constant conversation with God, to be aware of His presence with you throughout the day.

3. **Listen to Worship Music.** Worship music is a powerful tool for shifting your focus from your problems to your God. It can lift your spirits, it can renew your mind, and it can usher you into a place of peace and praise. Create a

playlist of your favourite worship songs, and listen to it while you are working, while you are exercising, or while you are driving. Let the music wash over you and remind you of the goodness and the greatness of God.

4. **Find a Community of Believers.** We were not meant to do this life alone. We need the support, the encouragement, and the accountability of other believers. Find a church, a Bible study, or a small group where you can connect with other women of faith. Share your struggles with them, pray for each other, and celebrate God's faithfulness together. This community will be a lifeline for you on your entrepreneurial journey.

5. **Practice Sabbath.** As we have already discussed, the practice of Sabbath is a powerful way to reconnect with God and to replenish your soul. Set aside one day a week to cease from your work, to rest, and to delight in the presence of God. This may seem impossible in your busy life, but I promise you, it is one of the most important things you can do for your business, your family, and your own well-being. When you honour the Sabbath, you are making a powerful declaration of your trust in God's provision, and you are opening yourself up to a deeper level of rest and renewal than you ever thought possible.

Making Time for Your Family

For the business mum, one of the greatest sources of both joy and guilt is her family. We love our children and our spouses more than anything in the world, and we want to be present for them, to nurture them, and to create a lifetime of happy memories with them. But the demands of our businesses can often pull us away from them, leaving us feeling torn, conflicted, and like we are failing at the most important job we have.

This is a struggle that I know all too well. I remember the heartbreak of missing my children's school events, of coming home late every night, and of feeling like I was a stranger in my own home. I remember the guilt that would wash over me every time I had to cancel plans with my children because of a work emergency. It was a painful and unsustainable way to live.

But I have also learned that it is possible to be a successful business owner and a present and engaged mother. It is not about achieving a perfect balance, which is a myth that only serves to make us feel more guilty. It is about being intentional, about setting boundaries, and about making the most of the time that you do have with your family. It is about choosing quality over quantity, and about creating moments of connection that will fill your children's hearts and your own.

Here are some practical strategies for making time for your family, even when you are busy:

1. **Schedule Family Time.** Just as you schedule your business meetings, you must also schedule your family time. Put it in your calendar, and protect it as fiercely as you would protect any other appointment. This could be a weekly family fun night, a monthly date night with your spouse, or a daily ritual of reading a bedtime story to your children. When you schedule your family time, you are sending a powerful message to your family, and to yourself, that they are a priority.

2. **Be Fully Present.** When you are with your family, be with your family. Put away your phone, turn off your computer, and give them your undivided attention. Listen to their stories, ask them questions, and be genuinely interested in their lives. Your children would rather have 15 minutes of your focused, loving attention than an hour of your distracted, half-hearted presence.

3. **Create Meaningful Rituals.** Rituals are the glue that holds a family together. They are the small, repeated actions that create a sense of belonging, of identity, and of security. You can create rituals around mealtimes, around holidays, or around everyday activities. It could be as simple as saying what you are grateful for around the dinner table, or as elaborate as a special tradition for each child's birthday. These rituals will become the cherished

memories that your children will carry with them for the rest of their lives.

4. **Involve Your Family in Your Business.** Your business does not have to be a separate and secret part of your life. You can involve your family in your business in age-appropriate ways. You can talk to them about your successes and your challenges. You can ask for their ideas and their opinions. You can even give them small jobs to do. When you involve your family in your business, you are teaching them valuable lessons about work, about money, and about pursuing your dreams. You are also giving them a sense of ownership and of pride in what you are building.

5. **Let Go of the Guilt.** Guilt is a useless and destructive emotion. It does not make you a better mother, and it does not help your children. It only serves to steal your joy and to keep you stuck in a cycle of self-recrimination. So, I want to give you permission to let go of the guilt. You are doing the best you can, and that is enough. Your children do not need a perfect mother; they need a happy and a loving one. So, be kind to yourself, celebrate your wins, and focus on all the ways that you are a great mum.

Creating a life of enjoyment is not about adding more to your already overflowing plate. It is about being more intentional with the time that you have. It is about infusing your days with moments of joy, of connection, and of meaning. It is about building a life that is not just successful, but also deeply satisfying. It is about remembering that you are not just a business owner; you are a human being, a child of God, and a woman who is worthy of a life that is filled with laughter, with peace, and with abundant joy. So, go ahead, make time for enjoyment. You deserve it.

CONCLUSION

Your Journey to Fearless Wealth Begins Now

We have come to the end of our journey together through the pages of this book, but for you, a new journey is just beginning. It is a journey towards a life of fearless wealth, a life where you can be a present and loving mother, a passionate and successful business owner, and a devoted woman of faith, all without sacrificing your sanity or your soul. It is a journey towards a life that is not just successful, but also deeply meaningful, joyful, and abundant.

Throughout this book, we have explored the five foundational steps of the Fearless Wealth Blueprint, a proven system that has the power to transform your life and your business. Let us take a moment to recap the path we have travelled:

First, we learned about the critical importance of **Creating a Clear Vision**. Your vision is your roadmap, your North Star, and your anchor in the storms of life. It is a divine gift, a calling from God that gives your life purpose and direction. We discovered how to craft a vision that is not just about financial success, but that encompasses every area of your life, your family, your faith, your health, and your personal growth. A clear and compelling vision is the essential first step on your journey to fearless wealth.

Next, we delved into the power of **Taking Action**. A vision without action is just a dream. We learned how to break down our big goals into small, manageable steps, and how to build the discipline of consistency. We explored the importance of asking for help, of finding mentors, and of building a community of support. And we uncovered the secret weapon of the Christian entrepreneur: the power of prayer in our business decisions. We learned that success is not born from giant leaps of faith, but from the cumulative effect of small, intentional, and daily actions.

In our third step, we focused on **Strengthening Your Leadership Role**. As your business grows, so does your responsibility as a leader, both in your business and in your home. We explored the mindset of a kingdom leader, one who leads with humility, service, and integrity. We discussed the importance of building a team that shares your vision, of mastering the art of delegation, and of leading your family with love and with purpose. We learned that true leadership is not about power or position; it is about empowering others to become the best versions of themselves.

Then, we uncovered the transformative power of **Uplifting**

Yourself with Positivity. Your mindset is the lens through which you see the world, and it has the power to shape your reality. We learned how to challenge and overcome negative thoughts, how to rewire our brains for positivity through the practice of gratitude and affirmations, and how to cultivate a Christ-like mindset that is rooted in faith, hope, and an unwavering trust in God's sovereignty. We discovered that a positive mindset is not a passive state; it is an active and courageous choice.

Finally, we explored the essential, yet often neglected, practice of **Creating Time for Enjoyment**. We learned that enjoyment is not a luxury; it is a necessity for a healthy and balanced life. We discussed the biblical case for rest and enjoyment, and we explored practical ways to find joy in the small, everyday moments. We learned the importance of making time for our faith, for our families, and for ourselves. We discovered that a life of fearless wealth is not just a life of success; it is a life of deep and abiding joy.

My own story is a testament to the power of these principles. I have been in the darkest of valleys, facing financial ruin, betrayal, and overwhelming despair. I have known the crushing weight of guilt, the paralysing grip of fear, and the soul-crushing exhaustion of burnout. But I have also experienced the incredible grace and faithfulness of God, who met me in my brokenness and showed me a way forward. He gave me this blueprint, not just for my own life, but to share with you.

I want you to know, with every fibre of your being, that you are not alone in your struggles. The challenges you face are not a sign of your inadequacy; they are a normal and necessary part of the entrepreneurial journey. And more importantly, I want you to know that you have the power to overcome them. You have the strength, the resilience, and the creativity to build the business and the life of your dreams. You are a daughter of the King, and you were created for a life of purpose, of passion, and of fearless wealth.

This book is not just a collection of ideas; it is a call to action. It is an invitation to step out in faith, to embrace your calling, and to start building the life you were created to live. The journey will not always be easy. There will be challenges, there will be setbacks, and there will be moments when you want to give up. But you are not on this journey alone. God is with you, He is for you, and He will give you the strength you need for every step of the way.

You have everything you need to succeed. You have the vision, you have the plan, and you have the power of the living God within you. So, what are you waiting for? Your journey to fearless wealth begins now. Go, and build the life you love.

I'd love to end this book by asking you something honest:
Are you ready to flip the script on your life?

Losing my client was my catalyst... but yours can simply be this moment.
You now have the five proven steps to build fearless wealth AND achieve your dreams and you don't have to walk this journey alone. If you're ready to take the next step, I'd love to personally support you.

Your breakthrough might be one conversation away.

Book a free clarity call with me, and let's map out your next chapter together.

BOOK A FREE CALL TODAY

https://calendly.com/priscillamakopacoaching/discovery-call

Visit Our Website For More Info:
http://www.priscillamakopa.com/

Printed in Great Britain
by Amazon

4282fb1e-38d2-43d6-9bbd-ae9e5d8e4a63R01